The training of first aid at work

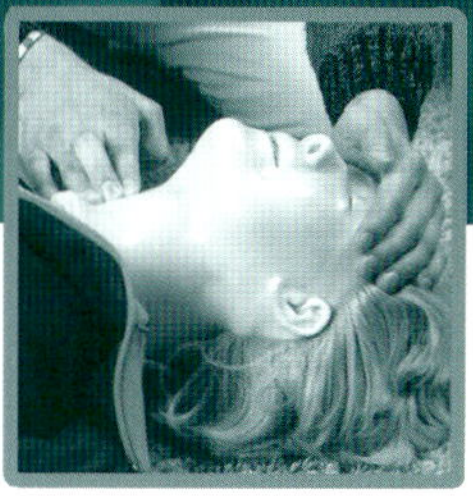

A guide to gaining and maintaining HSE approval

HSE BOOKS

© Crown copyright 2000
Application for reproduction should be made in writing to:
Copyright Unit, Her Majesty's Stationery Office,
St Clements House, 2-16 Colegate, Norwich NR3 1BQ

First published 1997
Second edition 2000

ISBN 0 7176 1896 X

All rights reserved. No part of this publication may be reproduced, stored in a retrieval system, or transmitted in any form or by any means (electronic, mechanical, photocopying, recording or otherwise) without the prior written permission of the copyright owner.

This guidance is issued by the Health and Safety Executive. Following the guidance is not compulsory and you are free to take other action. But if you do follow the guidance you will normally be doing enough to comply with the law. Health and safety inspectors seek to secure compliance with the law and may refer to this guidance as illustrating good practice.

Contents

- 1 *Introduction*
- 1 *Background*
- 1 *The law*
- 1 *Fees*
- 2 *Gaining approval*
- 2 Original approval assessment visit
- 3 Original approval monitoring visit
- 4 *Maintaining approval*
- 4 Post-approval monitoring visit
- 5 *Cancellations*
- 5 *Renewals*
- 5 *Appeals*
- 5 *Complaints*
- 6 *Appendix 1 –*
  Your Approval Status
- 6 Training
- 6 Administrative systems
- 6 Student certificates
- 6 Qualifications and experience of trainers
- 7 Qualifications and experience of assessors
- 7 Number of trainers and assessors
- 8 Number of students
- 8 Quality assurance plan
- 8 Training standards
- 8 Course syllabus: Lesson plans
- 9 Course duration
- 10 Final practical examination
- 11 Training equipment
- 11 Training premises
- 11 Assessment visit
- 11 Teaching standards
- 12 Assessment standards
- 13 *Appendix 2 –*
  Related training
- 13 Appointed person/emergency aid training
- 13 Specific hazard training
- 14 *Appendix 3*
- 14 HSE's contractor
- 14 Data Protection Act 1984
- 15 *Appendix 4 –*
  Sample lesson plan
- 16 References

Introduction

1   This guidance is designed to help you gain and maintain approval to carry out First Aid at Work (FAW) training. The Health and Safety Executive's (HSE) First Aid Approval and Monitoring Section (FAAMS) is authorised to issue and renew certificates of approval to FAW training organisations whose training and qualifications in FAW meet the requirements of the Health and Safety (First Aid) Regulations 1981 (the Regulations).

Background

2   Since 1 April 1997, field activities, relating to the approval of FAW training, have been provided by HSE's appointed contractor (the contractor). These activities had previously been undertaken by HSE's Employment Medical Advisory Service (EMAS).

The law

3   The Regulations[1] require that, in order to provide first aid to their employees who are injured or become ill while at work, employers must have suitable people, equipment and facilities. Regulation 3(2) says that:
'... for this purpose a person shall not be suitable unless he has undergone: such training and has such qualifications as the HSE may approve...', and 'such additional training, if any, as may be appropriate in the circumstances of that case.'

4   Under regulation 3(2) therefore, HSE will only approve FAW training and FAW requalification training. The Regulations are supported by an Approved Code of Practice.[2] You are advised to read both in conjunction with this guidance.

Fees

5   HSE will charge fees for the various elements of the approval process. HSE will inform you, in writing, of the details of those fees and the date they will become effective. After that, HSE will notify you of any changes to fees.

Gaining approval

6   To become a FAW training provider, you will need HSE's original approval. There is an original approval fee which covers all assessment activities carried out by HSE and its contractor, which include the original approval assessment visit and original approval monitoring visit.

7   You must first apply to:
    The Health and Safety Executive, First Aid Approvals and Monitoring Section, Grove House, Skerton Rd, Trafford M16 0RB
    Telephone: 0161 952 8322/8326/8280

8   FAAMS will send you an original approval questionnaire to complete. You will also be required to provide photocopies of the following documented information:
    - details of your administrative system;
    - a sample of the certificate to be issued to students;
    - personal portfolios of at least four individuals (two trainers and two assessors);
    - your quality assurance plan;
    - information about the standards of your first aid training;
    - details of your course syllabus, including at least three sample lesson plans, showing aims, objectives and outcomes;
    - a timetable for your four day syllabus;
    - a timetable for your two day syllabus (requalification), if applicable;
    - details of your final assessment procedure;
    - details about your training equipment;
    - information about your training premises.

9   Appendix 1 sets out the detail of information you are expected to provide. You must then send the completed questionnaire, photocopies of your information and the fee to FAAMS, who will acknowledge receipt of them if requested. FAAMS will then assess your application and inform you of the outcome. FAAMS will tell you if more information is required.

Original approval assessment visit

10 Once satisfied that you have provided a complete set of information,

FAAMS will promptly notify you that the contractor will be carrying out an original approval assessment visit. The purpose of this visit is to check the authenticity of all the information you have provided. The contractor will arrange with you a suitable time for a visiting officer to carry out the visit.

11 The visiting officer will provide FAAMS with a written report of the visit. FAAMS will consider the findings of that report and will then write to inform you of the outcome. Where you are required to make minor improvements, FAAMS will discuss with you how these can best be achieved.

12 If major improvements are needed, FAAMS will instruct the contractor to carry out an additional visit, once you have notified FAAMS that those improvements have been made. Please note that you will be charged a fee retrospectively for an additional visit.

Original approval monitoring visit

13 Once approval has been granted, FAAMS will send you a provisional certificate and a FAW training course notification form (MS79). You can complete either the MS79 or a form of your own choice. For each course you are intending to run, you must provide the following:
- the name and address of the training organisation on the certificate of approval;
- your approval number;
- the dates and times of the training course, including the final assessment;
- the course venue;
- whether it is a FAW training or FAW training requalification course.

14 This information must reach FAAMS at least four weeks before the start date of each training course. FAAMS will then instruct the contractor to arrange for a visiting officer to carry out the original approval monitoring visit. The visit will take place, where practicable, within three months from the issue of your certificate. This visit concentrates both on the assessment of your trainer(s) against the teaching standards set out in your application and the equipment and premises used for your training. You will need to ensure that the portfolios the trainer and two assessors, involved with the course, are made available for the visit.

15 The visiting officer will provide FAAMS with a written report of the visit. FAAMS will consider the findings of that report and will then write to inform you of the outcome. Where you are required to make minor improvements, FAAMS will discuss with you how these can best be achieved.

16 If major improvements are needed, FAAMS will instruct the contractor to carry out an additional visit once you have notified FAAMS that those improvements have been made. Please note that you will be charged a fee retrospectively for an additional visit.

Maintaining approval

Post-approval monitoring visit

17 Post-approval monitoring visits are carried out to established FAW training organisations to assess whether compliance is being maintained. The visit will look at all aspects of your training delivery. In particular, you will need to ensure that the portfolios of all your trainers and assessors are made available for the visit. If you employ a large number of trainers and assessors then you will be expected to provide a representative sample of portfolios.

18 Each organisation will receive at least one post-approval monitoring visit during the five year approval term. The number of visits each organisation will receive will be determined by the actual number of training locations used by the organisation. There is a fee for a post-approval monitoring visit for which you will be charged retrospectively.

19 FAAMS will notify the contractor when your post-approval monitoring visit is required. The contractor will contact you to arrange for a visiting officer to carry out this visit. (*Exceptionally, you may be visited unannounced to investigate a formal complaint either by HSE, its contractor, or both*).

20 The visiting officer will provide FAAMS with a written report of the visit. FAAMS will consider the findings of that report and will then write to inform you of the outcome of the visit. Where you are required to make minor improvements, FAAMS will discuss with you how these can best be achieved.

21 If major improvements are needed, the contractor will carry out an additional visit once you have notified FAAMS that those improvements have been made. You will be charged a fee retrospectively for an additional visit.

Cancellations

22 If you have to cancel either an original approval monitoring visit or post-approval monitoring visit, you must notify FAAMS giving at least three working days notice prior to the date of the visit. Failure to do this may result in a cancellation charge being levied.

Renewals

23 At least one month before the expiry of your current certificate of approval, you must apply to FAAMS if you want it to be renewed. You will be charged a renewal fee for your new certificate. You must send the fee with your application.

Appeals

24 You may decide to appeal against a decision not to issue you with a certificate of approval, where your approval status has been removed or where an additional visit is required. You must write to FAAMS (at the address in paragraph 7) with evidence to support your appeal. FAAMS will consider your appeal and inform you of its decision within ten working days.

Complaints

25 FAAMS will promptly investigate all written complaints.

Appendix 1
Your approval status

1   This Appendix is intended to help you to gain and maintain approval. It sets out the requirements of the approval process. Your application and any visit you receive will be assessed against these requirements.

Training

2   The purpose of FAW training is to enable people to practice first aid to the required standards to deal safely, promptly and effectively with injuries or illnesses which occur in the workplace.

Administrative systems

3   You must record the following information:
    - all dates of courses, including the names of trainers and assessors;
    - the name of each student;
    - the expiry date of each student's certificate.

4   This information must always be readily available for inspection by HSE or its contractor. Records must be retained for a minimum of *five* years. *Please note that FAAMS or the contractor are required to inspect only the above records. You do not have to provide, or be asked to provide, by either FAAMS or the contractor, any other records relating to your administrative system, as these may contain contain commercially sensitive information. (See Appendix 3 which refers to conflict of interest and confidentiality.)*

Student certificates

5   The following information must appear on the student certificate:
    - the title 'First Aid at Work';
    - a reference to The Health and Safety (First Aid) Regulations 1981;
    - the HSE approval number;
    - a statement confirming its validity for *three* years;
    - the date of expiry;
    - the signature of an appropriately authorised person from your organisation. Please note that a printed copy of the signature is acceptable.

Qualifications and experience of trainers

6 Your trainers must each have a personal portfolio which contains a:
- current FAW certificate, or if exempted, a current United Kingdom Central Council for Nursing (UKCC) registration certificate or proof of membership of the General Medical Council (GMC);
- certificate showing a training qualification. If the trainer does not have a training qualification, HSE will consider relevant experience detailed in the curriculum vitae;
- curriculum vitae or similar document detailing general skills, experience etc of training which has been applied to teaching and first aid in the workplace over the previous three years. During that time, the person must have conducted a minimum of *two* practical and *two* theoretical teaching sessions where they have been assessed by a qualified assessor.

Qualifications and experience of assessors

7 Your assessors must each have a personal portfolio which contains a:
- current FAW certificate, or if exempted, a current UKCC registration certificate or proof of membership of the GMC;
- certificate showing an assessor qualification. If the assessor does not have a assessor qualification, HSE will consider relevant experience detailed in the curriculum vitae;
- curriculum vitae or similar document detailing general skills, experience etc of assessing which has been applied to assessing and first aid in the workplace over the previous *three* years. During that time, the person must have conducted a minimum of *two* practical and *two* theoretical assessments, where they have been assessed by a qualified assessor.

8 Provided that they are able to demonstrate current experience and application of first aid skills through their personal portfolio, HSE accepts that the following trainers and assessors are exempt from holding a FAW certificate:
- a registered medical practitioner – proof of qualification is obtainable from the GMC;
- a first or second level registered nurse who is registered with the UKCC and has a current personal identification number (PIN Number).

Number of trainers and assessors

9 As an approved training organisation you must have at least two trainers and two assessors and must ensure that their personal portfolios are current through regular review.

Number of students

10 HSE recommends that you should allocate no more than 12 students to a trainer.

Quality assurance plan

11 You must have a quality plan for the delivery of your training and for the provision of premises and equipment. The quality plan must include a programme of regular review. Reports of those reviews must always be available for inspection and contain details of:
- the records of the assessments (at least annually) of your trainers and assessors and any outcomes;
- the people who assess the skills and knowledge of your trainers and assessors;
- student feedback on the quality of your training;
- your complaints procedure;
- the adequacy of your training equipment;
- the premises that you intend to use for training.

Training standards

12 First aid at work skills and knowledge must be taught and assessed in accordance with currently accepted first aid practice in the United Kingdom. At present HSE accepts the first aid management of injuries and illness, in as far as they relate to the topics to be covered in a FAW training course, as laid down:
- by the UK Resuscitation Council guidelines;
- by the European Resuscitation Council (ERC), where that agrees with the UK Resuscitation Council;
- in the current edition of the Voluntary Aid Societies – St John Ambulance, St Andrew's Ambulance Association and the British Red Cross;
- in other publications, provided they are based on sound medical, scientific research or are in line with the three above.

Course syllabus: Lesson plans

13 You must provide lesson plans for each syllabus topic. An example of a lesson plan is shown in Appendix 4. You must set aims, objectives and outcomes within each lesson plan, to measure a student's understanding of each of the syllabus topics. A combination of theory and practical tests will enable you to assess whether a topic has been understood by all the students. Only when you are sure this has been achieved should you move to the next topic.

14 On successful completion of the syllabus, each student must be able to demonstrate that they are able to:
- act safely, promptly and effectively with emergencies at work;
- use first aid equipment, including the contents of a first aid box;
- understand the duties of employers and the legal framework;
- maintain simple factual records on what they have done with regard to any treatment or management of an emergency;
- recognise the importance of personal hygiene in first aid procedures.

15 They must also be able to deal with a casualty who:
- requires cardiopulmonary resuscitation;
- is unconscious;
- is bleeding or wounded;
- is suffering from shock;
- is suffering from an injury to bones, muscles or joints;
- has been burned or scalded;
- has an eye injury;
- has been overcome by gas or fumes; or
- may have been poisoned or exposed to a harmful substance.

16 And, they must be able to:
- recognise major illnesses and take appropriate action;
- recognise minor illnesses and take appropriate action;
- manage the transportation of a casualty, as required by the circumstances of the workplace.

Course duration

17 A FAW training course must:
- last at least 24 contact hours. Contact hours include actual teaching and final assessment time, but exclude coffee and meal breaks;

- be run over a minimum of four days and a maximum of 13 weeks. If you choose to run a course over a period of weeks, each session must last a minimum of two hours.

18 A FAW requalification training course must:
- last at least 12 contact hours. Contact hours include actual teaching and final assessment time, but exclude coffee and meal breaks;
- be run over a minimum of two days and a maximum of six weeks. If you choose to run a course over a period of weeks, each session must last a minimum of two hours.

19 First aid at work certificates are valid for three years. However, a first aider can attend a course up to three months before the expiry date of their certificate. The new certificate will then be effective from that date.

20 If you require approval for requalification training you must have:
- a system that makes sure, before the training starts, that a student holds a current first aid at work certificate that will be valid throughout that training;
- a syllabus that includes reassessment of the student's knowledge and application of all FAW skills.

21 You must not combine FAW training courses with FAW requalification training courses. Additionally, all FAW training courses must 'stand alone' and not be included within the syllabus of non-first aid training courses.

Final practical examination

22 The final assessment must determine the student's ability to act safely, promptly and effectively when an emergency occurs at work and to deal with a patient who:
- requires cardiopulmonary resuscitation;
- is unconscious;
- is bleeding or wounded.

23 The approved training organisation must decide if a student has the required knowledge and skills. A student should only be given a FAW

certificate when the training organisation is satisfied that they are competent to safely deal effectively with first aid emergencies in the workplace.

24 The final assessment for each student must be conducted by two assessors who have not been involved with the teaching. If you are running more than one FAW training course concurrently at the same training premises, consider the most efficient use of your assessors.

25 You must provide a waiting area, separate from where the assessments are being carried out. You ned to ensure that students are not used as casualties during the final assessment.

Training equipment

26 Training equipment must include:
- current FAW publications for student's use during the course;
- other current reference literature;
- visual aids appropriate to the lesson plan;
- a ratio of one mannequin to four students in line with ERC guidelines;
- an adequate supply of clean dressings/bandages.

Training premises

27 Premises must be kept clean, tidy, in a hygienic condition and free from intrusive noise. If you do not have your own training premises, then training can be delivered elsewhere. However, as the training organisation, you must ensure each student is provided with:
- safe access and means of escape;
- adequate toilet facilities;
- adequate heating, lighting and ventilation;
- adequate and suitable floor space for practical sessions.

Teaching standards

28 Where a visit is undertaken to assess the delivery of your training, the visiting officer will consider the following.

Preparation and planning
- Is the classroom conducive for effective teaching and learning?
- Is the quality and detail of lesson plans sufficient and are the aims, objectives and outcomes clearly specified?

Effective delivery
- Is there an effective introduction to each topic?
- Is there adherence to the lesson plan?
- Are there adequate and sufficient training aids for the lesson?
- Is adherence to the overall timetable being maintained?

Trainer and student interaction
- Is the training being delivered producing good interaction between student and trainer?
- Are the students encouraged to participate in the lesson?
- Are outcomes achieved before moving onto the next lesson?

Assessment standards

29 If the visit is conducted during an examinations day, visiting officers will assess the following:
- Are assessors unobtrusive?
- Are clear instructions given to students?
- Is feedback given to students quickly and constructively?

Appendix 2
Related training

Appointed person/emergency aid training

1. This is not a statutory requirement and a HSE FAW-approved organisation must *not* state, verbally or in writing, that this type of training is a legal requirement. Equally, any certificates issued must not state or imply that this training is HSE-approved.

2. For those businesses where there is no requirement for an FAW-trained first aider, HSE strongly recommends that an appointed person(s) receives appointed person/emergency aid training, The training should last at least four hours and cover:
   - what should be done in an emergency;
   - cardiopulmonary resuscitation;
   - dealing with an unconscious casualty;
   - control of wounds and bleeding.

Specific hazard training

3. The time needed to provide such training must be in addition to that for a standard FAW course. Training in the management of specific hazards, such as oxygen, hydrofluoric acid or cyanide, must be provided as a distinctive separate course or at the beginning or end of a FAW course. Training organisations should ensure that they have instructors with the necessary skills, knowledge and competence to conduct such courses.

Appendix 3

HSE's contractor
Performance

1. HSE continually monitors all aspects of the contractor's service delivery against quality performance standards set out in the contract. To check that all contractor visits are carried out consistently nationwide and to the same exacting standards, FAAMS and the contractor use independent programmes of verification. These assess the performance of all the visiting officers against those standards.

Confidentiality

2. HSE's contractor is bound by the contract clause:
Knowledge of any information, working practices, techniques, intellectual properties, processes or drawings which are gained by the contractor in performing the services shall not be used, sold or otherwise disposed of to any part of the contractor's organisation or to any other business, enterprise or third party, nor shall the contractor make use of any such knowledge for commercial gain or for any purposes which may adversely affect the work, status or reputation of HSE or any other organisation.

Conflict of interest

3. HSE's contractor is bound by the contract clause:
The contractor must immediately identify all potential conflict of interest issues associated with the provision of the services by the contractor and shall promptly notify HSE of such issues as they arise. Should the contractor declare a conflict of interest then HSE reserves the right to use alternative service providers to meet its needs. Procedures for addressing and resolving conflict of interest will be agreed between both parties from time to time.

4. HSE has appointed an independent assessor to carry out assessment and monitoring activities where such conflicts are declared by the contractor.

Data Protection Act 1984

5. FAAMS will keep all records of approved training organisations in accordance with the above Act.

Appendix 4
Sample lesson plan
Perform cardiopulmonary resuscitation (CPR)
Time: two hours
Aim: To demonstrate effective adult CPR to a casualty that is unconscious, has no pulse and is not breathing.

Objectives | Tutor | Student

Objectives	Tutor	Student
Determine the risks to the first aider.	Describe and explain.	Question and answer.
Determine the level of consciousness.	Describe and explain.	Practical work using casualty/mannequin.
Establish correct head position.	Describe, explain and show method.	Practical work using casualty/mannequin.
Establish absence of breathing.	Describe, explain and show method.	Practical work using casualty/mannequin.
Establish that airway is clear.	Describe method.	Practical work using mannequin.
Explain how lungs are ventilated by artificial means.	Describe, explain and show method.	Practical work using mannequin.
Establish absence of circulation.	Describe, explain and show method.	Practical work using casualty/mannequin.
Explain how cardiac circulation is established, using chest compressions.	Describe, explain and show method.	Practical work using mannequin.
Explain the correct ratio between ventilations and chest compressions.	Describe, explain and show method.	Practical work using mannequin.
Explain how/when additional help is summoned.	Describe and explain.	Question and answer.

Outcome: Each student will have a practical assessment at the end of the lesson conducted by the trainer, covering the procedures listed in the lesson plan.

References

1 *The Health and Safety (First Aid) Regulations 1981* SI 1981/917 HMSO
ISBN 0 11 016917 4

2 *First Aid at Work. The HSE (First Aid) Regulations 1981. Approved Code of Practice and Guidance* L74 1997 HSE Books
ISBN 0 7176 1050 0

While every effort has been made to ensure the accuracy of the references listed in this publication, their future availability cannot be guaranteed.

Printed and published by the Health and Safety Executive   C60   01/01